On Fire For God

Restoring God's Plan and the Founder's Values to the Nation

Jim Dickson

On Fire For God:

Restoring the Founder's Values to the Nation

Cover design based on an Unsplash image by Ricardo Gomez Angel https://unsplash.com/photos/-98jVaVuGv0

Publishing services provided by DwightClough.com

Paperback ISBN: 9798731805469

2

Table of Contents

Setting

> *"Therefore everyone who hears these words of mine and puts them into practice is like a wise man who built his house on the rock"*
> *Matthew 7:24*

This commentary is being written on the one-year anniversary of dealing with Covid-19 in the U.S.

What is going on? It is rare to find unanimity of opinion among diverse groups of people. In fact, a sentence that includes the words "unanimity" and "diversity" has an oxymoron feel to it. However today we have near unanimity of opinion among diverse groups in the country on the matter of what is going on.

Conduct your own research. Ask people what they think is going on. On a recent FL vacation we asked that question of dozens of people from the East coast and Midwest and in all age groups. Over and over we heard folks first say they didn't really know, and then used words such as "weird," "odd," "different," "unusual," and "uncommon." Negativity was widespread.

I first noticed excess negativity fourteen months ago after reading a book by Senator Ben Sasse: *THEM: Why We Hate Each Other—and How to Heal.* The book was about people who were lonely and unhappy. That stimulated me to write a commentary on the reason so many people in the richest country in the world felt that way. I had no intention of writing more than one commentary when I wrote the first, *Mere Humanity.*

That writing dealt with our two natures; being made in the image of God and our sin nature acquired when Adam and Eve chose to go their own way in the Garden of Eden. The result, a sometimes latent but constant battle is going on within each individual and to some extent between individuals. No wonder people are lonely.

A second commentary, *Why Disasters?* was prompted by the emergence of Covid-19 and raised the question of whether Covid-19 might be retribution for disobedience to God's plan. After all, since the flood and Noah there were dozens of instances cited in the Bible of man's disobedience followed by retribution.

A third Commentary, *A More Excellent Way,* emphasized obedience to the Creator's word as an answer to Covid-19, especially obedience to the commandment to *"Love the Lord your God with all your heart and with all your soul and with all your strength and with all your mind, and love your neighbor as yourself." (Luke 10:27)*

A fourth commentary, *Living God's Plan,* discussed our addiction to power, pleasure, and prosperity as barriers to loving God and neighbors and as barriers to making the Creator's way normal living. A number of friends highly praised the book and said they would share it with others but few said they were going to change. It became apparent that knowing was only half the problem. "Doing" was the culprit. Why don't we do what we know we should do?

Then the light went on. In our culture, materialism was triumphing over spiritual values. Satan was winning the "Garden of Eden" battle. After a year of focusing on what was going on in the world I was confident of the diagnosis: As a culture we had become so addicted to power, pleasure, and prosperity that we did not have the will power to stand up for the country our Founders had bequeathed to us, "one nation under God with liberty and justice for all." I realized it would take a mighty power to reverse the course of our nation.

At this point, in what could only be an act of God, I noticed a book on a shelf in our bedroom, *The Incendiary Fellowship* by Elton Trueblood. Perhaps it was the red cover that caught my eye. On the first page I saw the signature of my wife's mother, a lady of great faith. She had written extensive helpful margin notes and underlining that dealt with the decline of spiritual values in the 1960's. I had read the book thirty years ago. Perhaps I should re-read it.

The author stated on the cover jacket that "I came to cast fire on the earth is one of the most neglected of Jesus' sayings." He continued, "the fire cast on the earth two thousand year ago by Jesus is flickering with alarming faintness." I began to feel this book was relevant to today and would help answer how to put faith into action.

The clincher was the words "mild Christianity" in the first chapter followed by the sentence, "This mild Christianity is largely separated from the Bible." Mild Christianity indeed, an apt description of the church today. As I proceeded to read the book I realized it was a treasure that provided a path for going from "knowing" to "doing" that I was looking for. The seeds for a fifth commentary were sown.

Not coincidentally at this time I had just finished reading three biographies. One was a biography of Dietrich Bonhoeffer[1]. Another was Nelson Mandela's autobiography.[2] The third was a new

---

[1] One of his famous quotes is appropriate for this commentary: *Only he who believes is obedient and only he who is obedient believes.*

[2] Nelson Mandela, *Long Walk to Freedom,* Back Bay Books, 1994

book about Winston Churchill[3]. It came to me that all three men had dealt with situations that called for incredible leadership to fight the age-old battle of good versus evil and the loneliness and unhappiness today were symptoms of the same battle of good versus evil. The difference, our battle involves spiritual death rather than physical killing. However all the battles of these leaders involved materialism dominating cultures with truth, values, principles and religious beliefs dying on the vine.

As I pondered the difference between wars involving physical killing and our unwillingness to fight for spiritual freedom a host of questions came to mind:

---

[3] *Winston Churchill*, 2020 autobiography by Herbert G. Nicholas, Rhodes Professor of American History and Institutions, University of Oxford, 1969–78.

o Have we gotten so immersed in our toys and joys that we have forgotten about *eternity*?

o Does our Christianity today serve as an *opiate* that prioritizes the here and now at the expense of the hereafter?

o Is our mild Christianity a religion that prioritizes *feel good* over "be ye therefore perfect even as our Father in heaven is perfect?"[4]

o Have we ceased to *challenge* non-believers for fear of being offensive?

o Why have we let what *people* want take priority over what God wants?

o Has the love we display in our relationship with others been so watered down that we neglect to *share the good news*?

---

[4] Matthew 5:48

o Do we not need the same boldness shown by Mandela, Bonhoeffer and Churchill and go on the *attack* against the enemy who is orchestrating our spiritual malaise?

o Do we care enough to *ignite* a fire?

This commentary, *On Fire for God,* is written in answer to the above questions with the realization that to live out God's plan (Commentary #4) requires individuals with a deep and abiding passion lived out in fellowship with others who are like-minded. Putting it bluntly, people on fire for the Lord in a fellowship on fire for spiritual truths.

Since Trueblood's writing opened the door for this Commentary it seems appropriate at this point to sneak a few quotes from his book as a type of appetizer for readers who might be frightened at the thought of internal spiritual fire.

"Those who try to follow the narrow way must expect to be part of a minority all of their lives." p. 26

"Though the New Testament describes a hot fire, we prefer the damp wick." p. 26

"Christian fellowship is never optional, if the life of Christ is to make an impact on the world." p. 28

"Mild religion cannot sustain itself because it cannot start even a tiny flame." p. 109

More quotes in a later chapter, "Fire." See also "Summary of Trueblood's Comments."

Darkness

What people value highly is detestable in God's sight. (Luke 16:15)

Our country is in a mess. That may also be true of many, most, or all nations today but our rich spiritual heritage passed down from our Founding Fathers suggests we should be a leader in knowing the way out of a muddle and in leading back to a solid foundation. How do we do start? Abraham Lincoln gave good advice, "If we could first know where we are and whither we are tending, we could better judge what to do and how to do it." Where are we and what do we need to do?

14

Our spirituality is a major problem. Materially we are blessed. Spiritually we are starving. The Bible warned of the dangers of this mismatch, "Man does not live on *bread* alone but on every *word* that comes from the mouth of the Lord."[5] God's word is life giving.

As noted in the Declaration of Independence and affirmed in the Constitution that specifically prohibits "laws respecting the establishment of religion," our Founders emphasized spirituality and believed in a Creator. Spirituality is in our nation's genes. However having the ability to do something is of no value unless the ability is utilized and part of the daily rhythm of the culture.

The spirituality of the Founders is no longer part of the daily rhythm of our culture. This is a topic worthy of extensive treatment but for this commentary a statement by Dr Andy Tix in *Psychology*

---

[5] Deuteronomy 8:3 & Matthew 4:4

Today is sufficient, "American adults (are) less likely to be religiously affiliated and to believe in God than they were previously." His reasoning, "The rise of self…and the decline of awe." A very astute observation. We have elevated "I," "me," "my" at the expense of awe of God.

Why is this happening? One reason is failure to pass on the basics of spirituality. There is widespread criticism today of the quality of public education in this country. A major reason cited is the failure to teach the basics in all disciplines, thus leaving graduates ill-equipped to function effectively in society. The same principle applies to spirituality. An overwhelming number of churches[6] today have failed in the past 60 years to teach spiritual basics such as the Genesis creation story, the Ten Commandments,

---

[6] This Commentary does not attempt to discuss teachings in synagogues, mosques and other religious forums.

the Sermon on the Mount, and the Greatest Commandment(s).

The result of not knowing spiritual basics has a direct impact on the spiritual decline in the country and helps create a host of social problems. Material basics are important but materialism creates a never-ending desire for more that can only be satisfied by spiritual values. A quote from Blaise Pascal[7] says it well:

> *"What else does this <u>craving</u>, and this <u>helplessness</u>, proclaim but that there was once in man a true happiness, of which all that now remains is the <u>empty</u> print and trace? This he tries in vain to fill with everything around him, <u>seeking</u> in things that are not there the help he cannot find in those that are, though none can help, since this infinite <u>abyss</u> can be filled only with an infinite and immutable object; in other*

---

[7] Blaise Pascal's Pensées (New York; Penguin Books, 1966. p. 75).

Craving, helplessness, empty, abyss—
sad words. This is not to suggest that a
return to teaching the basic will automat-
ically solve our problems because for
generations we have substituted man's
ways for God's ways. As a result and as
discussed in *Living God's Plan* we have
become addicted to an excess of power,
pleasure and prosperity and other forms
of material excess the world has to offer.
Spiritual addictions can be very subtle
and devious.

For example, years ago I greatly enjoyed the song *I Did it My Way* especially
when sung by Frank Sinatra.

The song is captivating and by itself
relatively harmless but not when the
world continually provides a steady diet
of such songs that suggests man's way is

superior and satisfying. Addictions give temporary pleasure but are a path to darkness. This is not the Creator's plan.

It is time for a reality check. We have strayed far from God's fruit of the Holy Spirit, "love, joy, peace, patience, kindness, goodness, faithfulness, gentleness, and self-control."[8] Instead too often we accept the darkness that comes with the works of the flesh; "sexual immorality, impurity and debauchery; idolatry and witchcraft; hatred, discord, jealousy, fits of rage, selfish ambition, dissensions, factions and envy; drunkenness, orgies, and the like."[9]

In a later chapter we will discuss how we can have the fruit of the Spirit. For now it is enough to recognize the danger of allowing materialism to replace spirituality and dominate daily living. Varia-

[8] Fruit of the Spirit, Galatians 5:22-23
[9] Works of the flesh, Galatians 19-20

tions of "I did it my way" is still often Satan's well disguised trap.

What made man go astray? The answer was covered in the first commentary *Mere Humanity* and repeated in each of the commentaries. God made heaven and earth and all that is therein; made man in his image; placed man in charge of His creation; and gave instructions on how to live and care for His creation. Error number one began in the Garden of Eden, was common in Old Testament times, and was common through the ages. Deuteronomy 8:13-14 warns:

> *"when your herds and flocks grow large and your silver and gold increase and all you have is multiplied, then your heart will become proud and you will forget the Lord your God…"*

Going astray—man choosing to go his own separate way--continues today.

It is defiance of God's will. For convenience call it sin. Sin may arrive on the scene with a thrill but it always ends making things darker[10] because it separates us from God and from others.

Sin is so deeply ingrained in our culture today that it will require extreme action to cure our addictions. We will discuss sin and steps to restore God's plan but first a time-out.

------

[10] The author is guilty in thought, word, or deed of many of the sins specifically identified in these commentaries.

Time Out

So from now on we regard no one from a worldly point of view. (II Corinthians 5:16)

This Commentary deals with a major change in our culture because we as a culture are addicted to excess power, pleasure and prosperity. We are in a similar position to that of individuals controlled by addiction. Changing from bad to good involves a one hundred eighty-degree turnaround. We have no choice if we want life that is meaningful and fulfilling now and life everlasting when we leave this plane. The alternate for our culture is the same as that of any addict, change or continue on the path to oblivion.

Negative feelings abound when change is involved. Going to a dentist for a root canal is a good example. If we don't go, the pain will only get worse. If we go, the pain will be gone after a period of discomfort. The dentist will only be doing what needs to be done to replace bad with good and that is good riddance! We trade rot for repair, restoration and recovery. The same mindset will be required to say no to self and yes to the superhuman power that will be needed to free us from our addictions to going along doing what we feel comfortable doing.

This Commentary is written to facilitate the progress of replacing the bad (addiction to excess materialism) with the good (fruit of the Spirit). Because this commentary contains a number of comments some might find offensive, common sense suggests the author make clear his purpose, reasons, and mindset in writing.

Many of the comments are based on the experience of the author and his understanding of the Creator's plan that are the result of years of Bible reading, involvement in weekly Bible studies, thirty years consulting with a wide variety of churches on leadership development, and a personal experience of spiritual change.

The content is not intended to say "do this" or "this is how you should live." Rather it is to stimulate thinking on question that go to the heart of why we are here and what were we created to do. The author believes only the Creator knows His plan for others and that leaves no room or reason to criticize others.

One of the best ways we can help others is by example with emphasis on living out the commandments to love God and love our neighbors.

The commandment to "love your neighbor as yourself" includes all contacts including phone, mail, meetings and appointments, in stores, and just passing on the street. At a minimum, smile. At the other extreme, consider whether this person has a need God wants me to act on. My wife and I recently experienced this when we noticed a mother and two daughters sitting in the back row of the church as we were leaving. Recently evicted from her apartment for failure to pay rent she noticed cars in the parking lot and came in after praying for help. We asked the obvious question, Why did you come this morning? Her prayers were answered.

Many are not experiencing joy in their lives today because they are uncertain of what they were created to do.

This commentary is designed to stimulate thinking toward this end.

Many are not finding fulfillment in their daily routine and need motivation to think through how to find peace, joy, and happiness each day. This commentary is designed to stimulate thinking through the routine of daily living.

One of the most important reasons for our brief time on earth is to prepare for eternity. Just making this a priority would greatly improve our quality of life on earth.

The author is grateful for friends who helped me return to the path prepared for me and prays this Commentary will serve that purpose for others.

Leaders

"You must go to everyone I send you to and say whatever I command you. Do not be afraid of them, for I am with you and will rescue you," declares the Lord." Jeremiah 1:7b

Addiction is nothing new. What is new is recognizing we have a *cultural* addiction and then attracting courageous men and women who will commit to doing something about it. It will require leaders on fire for God. Godly fire is abhorrent to many and rightly so if the fire is not controlled. On the other hand fire is part of everyday life in many areas including for warmth, light, food preparation, and to purify.

Our materialism has become an addiction so strong many people no longer have the desire to stand up to the god of materialism. It will take time for such leaders to emerge. Where will the Jeremiahs come from today?

A good place to start is to consider the early church that despite constant persecution was so powerful it eventually led to a change in the culture of the Roman world. One of the leaders, the apostle Peter, wrote in a letter to churches,

> *You spent enough time in the past doing what you would like to do, when you lived in unbridled immorality, lusts, drunkenness, wild celebrations, drinking parties, and the abominable worship of idols. I Peter 4:3*

Peter went from denial[11] to being a man of courage who accepted the challenge to battle forces of evil. Imagine the reaction of the people who received his

___
[11] "I do not know this man" Matthew 26:72

letter. Imagine the reaction of people today as they begin to realize that what we like to do and have become accustomed to do is powered by a force that is a path to darkness. *Mere Humanity*[12] describes the battle taking place between our sin nature (our self-will) and our good nature that comes from being made in the image of God. To understand our situation today it is worth reviewing the creation story again.

In the beginning "God created man in His image,"[13] placed him in the Garden of Eden, and said "you must not eat from the tree of the knowledge of good and evil, for when you eat of it you will surely die."[14] Soon Satan, the great deceiver came along and told Eve, "you will not surely die"[15] but Adam and Eve

---

[12] Commentary #1 (Jim Dickston, *Mere Humanity*, Amazon, 2019.)

[13] So God created man in His own image…male and female He created them. (Genesis 1:27)

[14] Genesis 2:17

[15] Genesis 3:4

"did eat of the fruit."[16] As the result of Adam choosing evil over good, his descendants inherited a trait of disobedience that remains today. No matter how hard we try we can't reverse that decision. The list of notables today who stumble and fall, let alone the lives of all of us, bears witness to how weak we are to resist the tempter.

God could have given His power to resist Satan to Adam and Eve but then we would have a world of 7 billion gods today, an intolerable situation. What did He do?

Four thousand years ago He called a people. He told Abram, later called Abraham,

> *I will make you into a great nation*
> *and I will bless you; I will make*
> *your name great, and you will be a*

---

[16] Genesis 3:6

blessing,… and all peoples on earth will be blessed through you.[17]

He then sent His chosen people to Egypt for 400 years to learn obedience and had Moses lead them to the promised land. It didn't work, disobedience followed disobedience. Seventy years in exile didn't work. At last God sent His son whose death on the cross made God's superhuman power available so that "whosoever believeth in Him should not perish but have everlasting life."[18]

Through the ages many have believed and stood up to bring light to their world. The Emperor Constantine largely ended Christian persecution in 325 A.D. The Reformation leaders in the 16th & 17th centuries battled powerful forces to make God's word available to the masses. The Founding Fathers of the

---

[17] Genesis 12:2-3

[18] John 3:16 b

31

United States pledged their lives, fortunes and sacred honor to gain freedom for the people and unite the states in a war against the strongest country in the world.

Strong leaders continue to have the courage to stand up for what is right as noticed earlier in "Setting." Dietrich Bonhoeffer was such a person. He could have enjoyed the safety of remaining in England but lost his life by choosing to return to his native land whose leaders were killing millions of people. Nelson Mandela said that 300 years of slavery for the people of South Africa was too long. He refused freedom, spent 30 years in prison, and was only released when there was freedom for his people. Winston Churchill at an age when men thought of retiring accepted responsibility to lead his country in a war most people felt was hopeless against a foe that in two years had conquered nearly all the continent of Europe. These leaders were on fire for God.

Brave men and women are needed today to give leadership in the battle to overcome our culture's addiction to materialism and to restore spiritual values. It is not easy for an individual to overcome an addiction. It is a huge problem for a culture to admit to addiction and then to follow through with necessary changes.

Addictions are powered by a sin nature that wants to be god. We all have that nature. It is powerful. The apostle Paul described the problem well, *"That which I do, I do not want to do; that which I want to do, I do not do. Woe is me."* Later he asked, "Who will set me free from the body that give me this death? Thanks to God, he does it through our Lord Jesus Christ."[19]

---

[19] Romans 7:19-25 paraphrased.

This superhuman power is still available today as will be discussed later in the Epilogue to this Commentary. It is a power that is essential for leaders if our culture is to get out of the "works of the flesh" darkness and return to the light of the "fruit of the spirit." Superhuman power enables leaders and believers to be on fire for God and living His plan.

The next step is for leaders to have a realistic understanding of how far we have strayed from God's way.

Obedience

"Do not think that I have come to abolish the Law or the Prophets; I have not come to abolish them but to fulfill them." Matthew 5:17

Obedience is not a popular subject today. The common practice is to *stray* from rather than *stay* with God's plan for man. For several reasons there is a reluctance to even discuss the need to obey His plan.

One reason is our old nature's resistance to criticism. The current excuse is to say your criticism offends me. Topic closed! Another reason is that obedience frequently involves the topic of morality, what personal conduct is right and what is wrong. The prevailing view in our culture is that morality is a personal matter that does not require adherence to someone else's code of conduct.

A third reason obedience is not commonly discussed today relates to Thomas Paine's frequently quoted observation that, *"A long habit of not thinking a thing is wrong gives it a superficial appearance of being right."* We have strayed so far and so long from God's plan for man that key factors in what was thought wrong are now accepted as right.

Finally the law of the land is part of the equation. In a democracy people normally feel they have authority to establish the codes of conduct on morality. The past sixty years have seen seismic shifts in the United States on matters involving sexual conduct, marriage, speech and addictive substances. In many cases the new laws simply engrafted prevailing moral practices into law. Our human nature has little or no trouble codifying what the majority wants without regard to the *Laws of Nature and Nature's God.*

Our Founders relied on the Laws of Nature and Nature's God in the foundational documents for our country. "Laws of Nature" establish standards of right and wrong. "Nature's God" recognizes oversight of creation. Human nature, which tends to start with what man wants, therefore often finds itself in opposition to the Laws of Nature and Nature's God.

Historian Robert R. Reilly has written an excellent book on the intent of the Founders regarding Laws of Nature and Nature's God.[20] He warns of the danger of human standards,

> *As soon as one moves from the rational "Laws of Nature and of Nature's God" to the one making human will that standard, one is*

---

[20] *America on Trial,* in Defense of the Founding, Ignatius press 2020.

headed for Leviathan.[21] We are now enduring such a transformation in the United States where political rule is becoming increasingly arbitrary.

The Laws of Nature and Nature's God are not suggestions. God gives commands. Therefore to know what we are doing wrong we must start with God's standards of what is right. An honest appraisal of our culture today would lead to the conclusion we are going in the opposite direction from what He intended. What is this plan? In what ways are we straying?

While our Founders relied on the *Laws of Nature and Nature's God,* we would benefit by a reminder of the standards that flow from these laws such as: God made man in His image and said rule over all the earth; "a man will leave

---

[21] A Bible sea monster; anything of huge size; gigantic, formidable (Chambers Concise Dictionary)

his father and mother and be united to his wife and they will become one flesh"; they shall be fruitful and increase in number, fill the earth and subdue it."[22]

His commandments also include: no other Gods, no idols, don't misuse God's name, observe the Sabbath, honor your Father and Mother; no murdering, adultery, or stealing, giving false testimony, or coveting what belongs to others[23] and of course the Greatest Commandment to love God wholeheartedly and love your neighbor as yourself."[24]

Christ said he came "to fulfill the law." At the same time his standards for daily living in the Sermon on the Mount took the harshness out of the law. The standards include a new attitude toward the poor, those who mourn, the meek, and those who hunger and thirst for

---

[22] Quotes from Genesis 1 & 2

[23] Deuteronomy 5:7-21 summarized

[24] Matthew 22:37

righteousness. He said be merciful; strive for purity, bless the peacemakers and those persecuted because of righteousness.[25] He reversed man's ways when He said it is better "to give than to receive"[26], and "I came to serve not to be served"[27].

Finally Christ highlighted the importance of obedience when he told His disciples to go make disciples and teach them to observe all my commandments.[28] Obedience to all God's commandments is still His plan.

Are we *staying* with or *straying* from these standards? This has practical importance as numerous surveys show a close correlation between mental well-being and obedience. We recognize the value of periodically checking on our physical condition; our spiritual condi-

---

[25] Matthew 5:2-11 summarized

[26] Acts 20:35

[27] Matthew 20:38

[28] Matthew 28:18-20 Summarized

tion is at least as important. The situation calls for spiritual examinations not unlike a physical exam. This gives rise to a conflict—we are often blind to our spiritual faults but reluctant to involve others in discussing them. This topic is covered in "Action," steps 5 & 7. At this point it is enough to know we need help.

Since God's standards provide a benchmark for measuring spiritual health there is a need for an honest assessment on deviations from these standards, both in regard to our culture and our personal lives.

As for our culture, the greatest commandment is to love our neighbor as ourselves, but how often do we speak ill of others? those we disagree with? those with different political beliefs than ours? How often are our Presidents and others placed in authority over us vilified by millions of citizens and by the media? Justified or not is not the point—speaking ill of others is a violation of God's greatest commandment. Disagree yes, criticize yes, but speak the truth in love. God makes no exceptions to this command.

There are several reasons for this command. Hating is a stain on our culture, it is a work of the flesh, it adds to darkness, and it rarely if ever changes the other person. Hating of government officials has the added negative of tearing down the house we all live in. This one command, "love your neighbor" if observed would have a dramatic impact on the quality of life in our culture.

How is our culture doing in regard to the other part of The Greatest Commandment, love for God? One measurement of love for God is church membership. A recent Gallup survey[29] showed that membership in a church, synagogue, or mosque had declined in

29 *"U.S. Church Membership Down Sharply in Past Two Decades,"* Gallup survey, April 18, 2019

just the last 20 years from 70% of the population to 50%. We are at the point of idolatry, of being primarily a materialistic culture.

Perhaps the biggest change in our culture's moving away from God relates to family matters. In the last twenty years the judicial system has gone from labeling certain conduct relating to marriage illegal, because it contradicted God's word, to making it illegal to even suggest this conduct is wrong. Similarly sexual behavior is a powerful force that cries out for open discussion and wisdom in decision making involving God's plan. This has not been the case. A handful of unelected judges have reversed moral practices without regard to consequences.

The net effect is that the family unit is no longer a solid building block for raising up a generation imbued with values essential for spiritual growth. We have replaced values that provide meaning to life with rampant materialism that demeans. Family values are a glue that bond us as a nation and assure a constant flow of generations that know right from wrong. Family values are the GPS that guides a culture upward. They are the balm that calms when threatened by turmoil. We must have leaders who will not tolerate apostasy and who will be leaders in purifying our culture.

Nearly everything said about the deterioration of our culture is the net result of individuals succumbing to their old nature's desire to "be like God." Formally this was primarily driven by individuals falling to the temptation of the tempter. Today this process has accelerated, aided by social and commercial media, by an educational system that in too many disciplines substitutes feeling for facts, and by government officials who pander to our human desire for power, prosperity, and pleasure.

Can we really improve on God's plan for genders, families, worship, civility, caring, honesty, purity, serving, unselfishness, and love?

Watch TV, read newspapers, watch movies and the norm is to trumpet the message of reprobate minds. Violence, greed, sexual immorality, dishonesty, hate, anger, jealousy, idolatry, and on and on. Why do they do this? Primarily because it is easier to reach the target audience by feeding man's old nature than by spending the time and effort required to communicate what is kind, good, admirable, lofty and energizing, and live at the level where we were meant to live.

The Old Testament contains many examples of retribution for disobedience and there is a widespread feeling that the New Testament story of Jesus coming on earth brought love in a way that meant there would be no more retribution. Not true. Just one example. Acts 5:1-10 tells the story of Ananias and Sapphira who sold property but "lied to men" and "kept for yourself some of the money you received." Both "fell down and died" and "great fear seized the whole church and all who heard about these things." We too are a people who are lying about ownership, about who owns the world and the owner's plan for the world. Perhaps that is why disasters keep coming.

Jesus said He, "came to cast fire upon the earth"[30], and He said "blessed are the pure in heart for they shall see God"[31]. Fire and purifying can go together and be extremely beneficial. Our Founding Fathers appropriated this fire and went on the attack to defeat a powerful external enemy. We need this purifying fire in order to see God's plan

---

[30] Luke 12:49
[31] Matthew 5:8

more clearly and go on the attack in the power of the Holy Spirit to defeat our internal enemy, our addiction to excess power, prosperity, and pleasure that neutralizes our willingness to obey His plan for man.

Isaiah said, "I heard the voice of the Lord saying, 'Whom shall I send? And who will go for us?' And I said, 'Here am I. Send me!'"[32]

Who will be the Isaiahs today?

---

[32] Isaiah 6:8; Luke 12:41 tells us Isaiah "saw Jesus' glory."

Fire

"I came to cast fire upon the earth." (Luke 12:49)

The purpose of this Commentary is to stimulate individuals, groups, churches, and related organizations to use purifying fire to carry out God's plan for man and return our nation to the Founder's roots.

Since creation and the fall of man, the history of the world, of nations, and of individuals has been one of ups and downs, from good to bad, lasting anywhere from days to months and years.

It is time to make the "ups" permanent.

Not only are we missing out on the blessings that come from obedience but, as Luke 16:8 reminds us, "What is highly valued among men is detestable in God's sight."

Our culture needs to be purified. This need is not something new. There have been purifying revivals many times in the past that lasted for months and years especially in the 18th and 19th centuries. We can learn from these revivals but why not have long lasting or even permanent cultural change this time?

Our culture is so decadent it will take a herculean effort to effectively deal with our disobedience. Another word for herculean is "superhuman." That gives a clue as to where the power must come from.

Since a culture is composed of people, changing a culture requires a change in people, a change in their hearts. The author's commentary *Living God's Plan* discusses twelve step programs and the success they have found in changing lives. These programs emphasize belief in a higher (superhuman) power, confession of sin, accountability through a sponsor, support groups, and service to others. A similar process is appropriate for culture change.

The *Setting* chapter noted that this commentary, emphasizing knowing what to do and doing it, was inspired by reading the book *The Incendiary Fellowship* by D. Elton Trueblood[33]. It would seem prudent then to use his book[34] and especially the last chapter as a resource for what will be required to make God's plan regnant in the hearts of man today.

The guidance that follows then does not originate from this author. It is a

---

[33] The Incendiary Fellowship, Elton Trueblood, 1967, Harper and Row

[34] Although I have experienced life change I claim no superior expertise for making cultural change. The next best step is to rely on the source that stimulated this commentary.

combination primarily of scriptural passages relating to the power of the early church to make cultural changes and Trueblood's incisive comments on these biblical passages.

What then are the ingredients in Trueblood's recipe for reversing the course of our nation? Not surprisingly they place strong emphasis on purifying individuals, the church, and the nation. What better way to connect with God than through purity? His word states in Matthew 5:8, *"Blessed are the pure in heart, for they shall see God."* As we rapidly move in a direction opposite God's way, is it any wonder that we have come to live in a post-Christian era with seemingly insolvable problems? Day after day can go by without even hearing the name of God, let alone discussions on what His word says is right.

The last chapter of *The Incendiary Fellowship* begins with Christ's warning, "I came to cast *fire* upon the earth."[35] True-blood notes the fire would involve something *very big* as Christ said three times in Matthew chapter 12 alone.[36] Christ also said it was for *all*, that is not a select few, and He said, "the good news of the kingdom of God is preached, and every one enters it *violently*,"[37] the ultimate alternative to mildness. Trueblood notes the difference between baptism by water and by fire is not small, "it is total." Water *cleanses*, fire *ignites* and consumes.[38]

The chapter goes on to note Christ's reference to fire was followed in the Book of Acts[39] by the Pentecost experience of the disciples "all gathered together in one place...they saw what seemed to be tongues of fire." This led

---

[35] Luke 12:49

[36] Verses, 6, 41 & 42

[37] Luke 16:16

[38] Ibid p 106

[39] Acts 2:1-4 summarized

52

to a community bonded "with glad and generous hearts."[40]

The chapter also places a strong emphasis on *fellowship*. A quote explains why:

> *Much of the uniqueness of Christianity, in its original emergence, consisted of the fact that simple people could be amazingly powerful when they were members one of another.*

My wife and I were recently reminded of the importance of group fellowship when a friend commented that a recently deceased mutual friend, a life-long Episcopalian, had "come on fire" late in his life at a Saturday morning group discussion at our home as part of a Faith Alive weekend. Bill, who "came alive" that morning, told us years later that after many years of going to church

----

[40] Acts 2:46

all it took for him to change was seeing ordinary people freely talking about the Bible. Bill then joined and remained in a weekly Bible study the rest of his life. His joy as a new believer was a refreshing reminder to the rest of us of the difference between living man's plan and God's plan.

Another Trueblood comment related to fellowship:

> *It is almost impossible to create a fire with one log, even if it is a sound one, while several poor logs may make an excellent fire if they stay together as they burn…*

He also notes:

> *Many when they tell frankly how their lives have been changed, refer to the faith and witness of some wholly obscure person who has been the instrument of ignition.*

Trueblood's book provides a blue-print for revival: [41]

> *Evangelism occurs when people are so enkindled by contact with the central fire of Christ that they, in turn <u>set others on fire</u>.*

> *The fact that we are dealing with holy things does not mean that piety can take the place of costly <u>competence</u>.*

> *We tend to interpret our vocation as that of husbanding the little flame in the effort to keep it flickering a little longer. What we ought to know is that <u>a flame cannot</u>, in its very nature, <u>be contained</u>.*

(If it goes out, don't blame the flame.)

---

[41] Ibid pp. 111-121 See also, Appendix "*Summary of Comments*

We shall not long continue to be service-centered if we cease to be <u>Christ-centered</u>.

Most contemporary Christian leadership are <u>rational evangelicals</u>, who recognize no difficulty whatever in being both hardheaded on intellectual problems and <u>warmhearted</u> in their <u>love of Christ</u>.

What we need is <u>quiet fanatics</u>.

<u>Low expectancy</u> is sin.

The church is meant to be an <u>incendiary fellowship</u> and nothing less.

Do we have a choice? I think not. Even before Covid-19 the shift from spiritual to materialism found us coasting down a slippery slope in the opposite direction from God's plan leaving behind the quality of life the Founders, and God, intended for us. Instead we are heading for the sea of despond with all its despots; despair, destruction and death without hope.

Covid can be a curse or a blessing. A curse if we think a cure for Covid solves all our problem, for a cure will ignore our addiction and will mean a return to the works of the flesh and the sins of the world.[42] A blessing if we see it as a wake-up call to cure our addiction and make God's plan our plan for life that is meaningful, fulfilling, abundant, and everlasting.

Our addiction is the problem. It is destroying our willingness to obey God's commands.

How then do we proceed to use the purifying fire Christ came to *"cast upon the earth"*?

---

[42] See Chapter 2 Darkness

Blunt Appraisal

What good will it be for someone to gain the whole world, yet forfeit their soul? Or what can anyone give in exchange for their soul?
Matthew 26:16

As a culture do we really need to change? We are considered a *superpower* by much of the world and are often relied on as a peace-maker, a role requiring enormous strength. We are a nation offering a wide variety of *recreational* opportunities as show-cased in the Olympics every four years. And we are an *affluent* country with a standard of living as high as any nation in the world. Why should we change?

Re-read those three sentences again. They are about *power, pleasure,* and *prosperity,* factors mentioned repeatedly in this commentary but always in connection with the word "excess." These are worthy aspirations but they become addictives when they focus inward and control our decision-making. Then they become gods.

When controlled by addictives "'my" welfare becomes pre-eminent and the Greatest Commandment, love for God and neighbor, takes second place. When that happens materialism triumphs over spirituality and we end up living "by *bread* alone" instead of "every *word* that comes from the mouth of God."[43] When that happens we end up a culture suffering from spiritual malnutrition, the same problem faced by every person addicted to a substance or habit.

---

[43] Matthew 4:4

We are a culture at the point where we no longer have the will power to admit we are addicts on a path to darkness. What will be the cost? In one word, *freedom*! A freedom so valuable that our Founders pledged their lives, fortunes, and sacred honor to provide it. They wrote a constitution for a people "endowed by their Creator with certain unalienable rights" including life, *liberty,* and the pursuit of happiness." Generations for 240 years have safeguarded these rights. Will we break trust with those who gave us this precious heritage?

Benjamin Franklin recognized the danger we are in. When asked what kind of government the new nation would have he said, "a republic if you can keep it." We are losing the freedom they fought to give us because the institutions of the country by and large now function for the benefit of those in power instead of for the people. Some examples of loss of freedom.

Government at all levels. A primary goal for many if not most elected officials is to get re-elected. This requires giving voters what they want (to get their votes) rather than to vote for what people need. A prime example is the current 1.9 trillion aid package related to Covid recovery that contains less than 10% for covid relief.

Big business is driven by meeting the needs of people and has been a major factor in the welfare of our country. However, and especially in this hi-tech era, there is an increasing trend to monopolize a market and drive out competition. Power corrupts.

Our *educational* system. Core disciplines are increasingly neglected. Feeling is replacing facts as the basis of truth. Educators use their power to teach the ideology they favor with little tolerance for opposing viewpoints. Teacher benefits often prevail over pupil needs. Topics with far reaching consequences such as sex education are taught by those ill prepared to teach the subject.

Churches have fallen into the same trap as schools in failing to teach core curricula. Do young people memorize the Ten Commandments, The Greatest Commandment(s), that basic hymn, "This is My Father's World"? As for adults, teaching God's plan on matters such as pre-marital sex, adultery, divorce, and transgenders is often neglected because it risks alienating members. A pastor friend said he felt "we who are key church leaders have failed" and he continued, "The world is more effective at discipling (to a world view) than we are." The result? Today the average church produces just three conversions a year.

What about the *common man* including your author? We aren't much different except in degree. I had an epiphany for a couple weeks following a (minor) covid experience and realized I had drifted into letting many activities and situation enter my life that were not God's plan and there was extensive need to "clean up and throw out" mental and spiritual garbage. As I realized I had slowly come to the point of accepting the world's values I realized this was true of the world and the reason for the tension and turmoil rapidly becoming the norm for our country. I felt like a seaman on a ship who had fallen asleep on his watch, a ship headed for a rocky coast.

Freedom of religion

The matter of freedom of religion requires special attention, especially as it relates to the educational system. The enemy has had a field day in regard to education. The Constitution states "Congress shall make no laws respecting an establishment of religion, or prohibiting the free exercise thereof…" For the next one hundred years mention of God continued to be an integral part of public education. Then the courts slowly began to tighten the noose until today teaching about God is totally banned.

Children attend school some six hours a day, 180 days a year, for twelve years without hearing God mentioned. What is going on is brain washing, blatant humanism,[44] and is never what the Founders intended, especially with a Constitution that states the government could not "prohibit the free exercise of religion." No wonder we are a culture increasingly substituting man's ways for God's plan. We have gone from freedom of religion to freedom from any religion except humanism. Getting God back into our public school curriculum will be

------

[44] Humanism: "any system which puts human interests and the mind of man paramount, rejecting the supernatural, belief in God." Chambers concise dictionary 1997

very hard to change but it must change and must be a very high priority.

Your blunt appraisal

If the world were a university, and in many ways it is, and God was the final authority, and He is, what grade do you think we as a nation would get on *Living God's Plan*? A, B, C, D, or F?

Action

In the same way, faith by itself, if it is not accompanied by action, is dead. (James 2:17)

It is time to attack. To go on the offense. After years of complicity in allowing excess power, prosperity, and pleasure to distract us from God's plan for man it is time to act. It is time to ignite purifying fire in our hearts, fire that is needed to remove the dross from our lives of "man's way." How this happens will vary for each individual but the process will be similar to the biblical command, "But everything should be done in a fitting and orderly way." (I Corinthians 14:40)

1. Start by calling on *higher power*, Holy Spirit power to burn freely in hearts to achieve purity needed to see God.[45] Our human nature can't do it. The God of our fathers can. We are in the position of the addict who says, "Enough, this is not what I want. Help!" Fortunately help is available. We have a higher power who said, "Ask and you shall receive, that your joy may be complete."[46]

2. God's *love* must be evident each step of the way to unite us, to attract others to join us, and to make clear to deniers our purpose, for there will be many seeking to dissuade us. God's love precludes us from judging deniers but not from discerning their intent.

3. *Humility* will be very important. We are all "poor little lambs who have lost our way and gone astray." We have no right to be proud just because our eyes

---

[45] Matthew 5:8 Blessed are the pure in heart, for they shall see God.

[46] John 16:24

are open. We have only the right to drink at the fountain of mercy that God so generously provides.

4. The next step, *repent.* "If we confess our sins, he is faithful and just and will forgive us our sins and purify us from all unrighteousness."[47] We must make a drastic turn-around in that part of our lives that is not part of God's plan. Name it, confess it, give it to Him. Good riddance.

5. Identify a *supporter* for accountability, someone who has successfully dealt with addiction and who will speak the truth in love. We are partially blind to our own inadequacy, and our old nature does not want to admit it is "unable." The qualities of humility and repentance are not welcome in the house of our old nature, the house we are in the process of purifying, and these and similar quali-

---

[47] I John 1:9

ties will be fiercely challenged by the enemy within.

At this point it is worth pausing to consider the *Beatitudes*[48] as a resource. Much of God's plan for man is laid out in Genesis and other parts of the Torah/Pentateuch[49]. That wasn't going very well so God sent His son. One of the first events of Christ's ministry was the Sermon on the Mount with the Beatitudes. Just as the first Christians needed the Beatitudes at the start of their world changing mission, so we will richly benefit using them as a resource for changing our culture. They remind us to be poor in (man's) spirit, to be pure in heart and merciful, to hunger and thirst after righteousness, and more. It would require a separate commentary to do justice to this topic.

---

[48] Matthew 5:3-10 Figurately the word Beatitudes means, "What is your attitude?

[49] The Hebrew and Greek names, respectively, for the first five books of the Hebrew Bible

6. *We are not the first.* Remember others have gone before us, especially the Founders. We are in a position similar to the United States in 1862 when Abraham Lincoln was President. The United States were in a war. The Civil War was fierce. We are now in a fierce war. Lincoln's challenge is helpful for us on how to unite and secure commitment from people not wanting to be involved in war, especially for a cause they did not understand. He said,

> *We can succeed only by concert. It is not "can any of us imagine better?" but, "can we all do better?" The dogmas of the quiet past, are inadequate to the stormy present. The occasion is piled high with difficulty, and we must rise -- with the occasion. As our case is new, so we must think anew, and act anew.*

<blockquote>
We must disenthrall ourselves, and then we shall save our country.[50]
</blockquote>

Note the similarities. We too can only succeed "by concert," by being united. We too must "all do better." "We must think anew and act anew as our mission is new" (When was the last effort to totally change our culture?), "We must disenthrall ourselves" from what we want to what God wants.

Lincoln referred to the "dogmas of the past." Our dogmas of the past are the addictions that have led us down the path of excess comfort, pleasure and desire for power, quiet dogmas indeed. We are a people seduced and our neurons will be very difficult to change.

7. Build a *Team*. Christ provided a model. He trained his disciples and "they turned the world upside down." Trueblood gave advice on picking team mem-

---

[50] Abraham Lincoln, concluding remarks, Annual message to congress, December 1, 1862

bers that don't fit man's usual mold. He said, "*Simple people* could be amazingly *powerful,*" and "Even *obscure persons* can be used to set others on fire." But he cautioned, "Nothing can take the place of costly *competence.*"

8. Our battle will be *fierce*. The "cancel culture" faction and the movement to tear down statutes show how deep the feelings are against returning to the foundation of the Founders. We are talking about years of struggle. It will be a challenge just to unite people. Even though we are a people that "pledge allegiance to the flag of the United States of America" those words are frequently lip sync today. They are words often scoffed at. This must change, but first hearts must be changed.

9. Use *12 Step Programs* as a guide. They have proven to be very helpful in dealing with *individual* addiction and recovery but they also provide helpful

guidelines for dealing with *cultural* addiction. There are a variety of these programs. Pick one and use as a guide.

10. Initially *focus* on removing the dross of excess power, pleasure, and prosperity. Minimize spending time on issues. As our eyes open the enemy would like us to concentrate on specific issues and neglect our house cleaning. Issues tend to deal with specifics, and success from working with issues can give measurable results that give immediate satisfaction. On the other hand, character building is amorphous with immediate results nearly impossible to measure, but with results that multiply and are never ending. Make life-changing a priority. Christ's disciples are our model.

11. Never forget that *freedom* is part of the objective. The Founders wrote in the Preamble to the Constitution that life, *liberty,* and the pursuit of happiness were unalienable rights. However what is writ-

ten in the Constitution is not necessarily forever. Benjamin Franklin anticipated our present situation of judicial legislation, and when asked he wisely said, you have *"A republic, if you can keep it."* Richard R. Beeman, Ph.D. noted twenty years ago that freedom required *"active and informed involvement of the people.[51]"* How true!

Freedom was also highly valued by Abraham Lincoln. He widely studied the Founders' writings and in 1863 in his Gettysburg address he concluded,

> *this nation, under God, shall have a new birth of freedom—and that government of the people, by the people, for the people, shall not perish from the earth.*

12. Be alert for *evangelism* opportunities. Evangelistic programs are helpful but lukewarm Christianity won't do it.

---

[51] From an article written for the National Constitution Center

Trueblood said, "Evangelism occurs when people are so enkindled by contact with the central fire of Christ that they, in turn, set others on fire.[52]

13. Last but not least, if spirit led people made the Greatest Commandment their mantra today, a large proportion of our cultural problems would disappear.

There is no secret what God can do,

what He has done for others,

He can do for (and through) you.[53]

---

[52] Trueblood, ibid p. 122
[53] Stuart Hamblen song, 1949

Epilogue

Practicalities of living "on fire for God"

Many years ago when I graduated from law school I felt confident in my knowledge of the content of the law but realized I had received no training in the practicalities of being a lawyer. You may be feeling the same way about the practicalities of being on fire for God. The question always is, what do I do now?

Perfection

Seek perfection but as a practical matter know we will never attain it. When we stumble and fall, get up and get going again. Being perfect is a process.[54] The enemy wants us to be discouraged. God tells us to "be anxious for nothing."[55]

Purity

"Blessed are the pure in heart for they shall see God" is so simple it is easy to ignore. We worry about satellites disrupting the grids that make secular communications possible but since creation we have let impurity disrupt our communications with the Maker. Identifying sin and repenting is essential for the calling.

Greatest Commandment

Obedience to the Greatest Commandment is a narrow path for being "on fire for God." God made no exceptions to this command though more often today people are *not* loving God and neighbors. Obeying the Greatest Com-

---

[54] "So you, my follower, ought to be perfect, as your heavenly father is." (Williams) Matthew 5:48
[55] Philippians 4:6

mandment is a very practical way to reverse the direction of our nation.

Love[56]

God is the source of love and He has an unlimited supply. He not only wants to share love with us but He wants us to be partners in sharing His love. Love is a product of relationships. Every encounter with another person is an opportunity to increase the quantity and quality of love on earth. Partnering with God in spreading His life-giving love is one of His greatest blessings.

Loving neighbors

In this ministry *every person* God brings into our lives each day is our neighbor. Loving neighbors can become addictive. Simply smiling and greeting those we pass warms hearts. Rarely is there a negative response. Even if there is, we have joy in knowing "God's word

---

[56] In this Commentary when the word "love" refers to God's love, unconditional, other-centered love.

never returns void." A greeting given in love is an expression of God's word.

Loving God

God is always watching over us and is worthy of a loving response such as talking with Him, asking for wisdom, and expressing gratitude. Years ago it was common at church services to sing the Doxology,[57] "Praise God from whom all blessings flow." We would do well to bring that hymn back as a reminder of who is the source of all blessings.

We also show love for God by seeking His wisdom and thanking him for blessings. His blessings abound. One small example.

We have a Christmas cactus that blossoms several times a year (but not during the Christmas season.) It is now

---

[57] Doxology: "A hymn expressing glory to God." Interestingly the word doxology is not part of the thesaurus of my computer program.

in full bloom and when I looked at it I was in awe of its beauty of intricately formed pinkish-red flowers and in awe that this process recurred year after year. How could that pot of dirt with just periodic watering and sunshine continually produce such beauty?

Loving Encounter

As a practical matter many of those we are to love are folks we have turned our backs on because their agenda is not our agenda. A major problem in our mission of living on fire for God will be encounters with people who feel offended by our emphasis on God and His word. The depth of this problem is conveyed in a recent magazine article;

> *Have we then disregarded the eternal rules of order and right that Heaven has ordained?...We have driven (God) out of schools... and our culture...and we've let in other gods and served them. We have re-*

jected His ways and embraced the ways of immorality. We've called evil good and good evil…We've passed down rulings from Washington, D.C. that war against the internal laws of Heaven on human life, human nature, gender, marriage [and] we've indoctrinated our children against the ways of God.[58]

Can forces of evil that are so strong and so deeply entrenched be subdued by those on fire for God? Yes!

We have these promises: "Above all, love each other deeply, because love covers over a multitude of sins."[59] And, "the one who is in you is greater than the one who is in the world."[60]

God is waiting for His people to take the initiative in reversing the direction of

[58] Decision magazine, March 2021, pp. 9-11 Article by James Dobson that included a letter by Jewish Rabbi Jonathan Cahn to President Biden, pp. 9-11

[59] I Peter 4:8

[60] John 4:4

this country. Brave men and women have been needed to uphold God's plan since He presented His plan to Abraham over 4,000 years ago. The animosity to His plan today is hatred of God's standards so there is no reason for us to take it personally. Freedom is at stake. Man's plan allows man to set the standards. When that happens, what is right or wrong is determined by the strongest leader who will then issue decrees and set laws to assure continuation of control.

Resources

Changing our culture will not be easy. The war will be long and hard. So were the Revolutionary and Civil Wars. Today we need more people like Mandela, Bonhoeffer and Churchill who were on fire. I am inspired by my father who wrote a letter in November 1918, "I am in the scout platoon searching for machine gun nests." And by my brother who as a fighter pilot received one of our nation's highest awards for risking his life in "continuous bombing and strafing passes in support of beleaguered friendly units." He survived after an emergency landing. We need similar bravery in our battle.

As a practical matter, our choices are: Man pleaser or God pleaser?

If we choose to be God pleasers we will need power from on high in order to be on fire for God. Nothing less will give us the wisdom and power to remove our debilitating addictions and return to God's plan for man.

Receiving higher power

The Holy Spirit is the greatest resource we can have. God has made it exceedingly simple to have His spirit control our life. Talk to God. Tell Him you need help. Repent of sins you are aware of and give them to Him. Invite the Holy Spirit to take over your life and make you the person you were meant to be. Thank Him for sending His son that you might have abundant and everlasting life. Share this decision with someone you know who is a believer and ask for help on growing spiritually. Join a Bible believing church.

Now you are ready to join in the battle to restore this great nation to God's plan and the Founder's roots.

What will you do?

Summary of Trueblood's Comments in *The Incendiary Fellowship*

Comments

Christ came to "*cast fire* upon the earth."

Scripture envisions something *very big*.

The fire is for *all*.

Every one enters the kingdom *violently*

Water (baptism) *cleanses*, fire *ignites* and consumes.

Simple people could be amazingly *powerful*

Even *several poor logs* can make an excellent fire

Even *obscure persons* can be used to set others on fire

Evangelism results in *glad* and *generous* hearts

Evangelism occurs from people *setting* other people *on fire*

Nothing can take the place of costly *competence*

A *flame cannot*, in its very nature, be *contained*.

To be service-centered requires that we be *Christ-centered*

Individual reflection and/or group discussion:

Do you agree that there is a critical need for being "on fire"? If so, is it realistic to think this could happen?

What needs to happen in your life, your church, your small group to come on fire?

Describe a process that it would take for you to come on fire? For your church?

Who might take the lead?

In Early Spring

William Wordsworth

I heard a thousand blended notes

While in a grove I sat reclined,

In that sweet mood when pleasant
thoughts

Bring sad thoughts to the mind.

To her fair works did Nature link

The human soul that through me ran;

And much it grieved my heart to think

What Man has made of Man...